IN FOCUS: NATIVE AMERICANS

# NAVAJO

## HISTORY AND CULTURE

MARK STEWART



Cavendish Square

Published in 2026 by Cavendish Square Publishing, LLC
2544 Clinton Street, Buffalo, NY 14224



Website: cavendishsq.com



Portions of this work were originally authored by Amarie Kyle and published as *Navajo* (Spotlight on Native Americans). All new material this edition authored by Mark Stewart.



Publisher: Katie Kawa
Book Design: Lisa Miley

Portions of this work were reviewed by: Robert J. Conley, Former Sequoyah Distinguished Professor at Western Carolina University and Director of Native American Studies at Morningside College and Montana State University.

Photo Credits: Library of Congress (4 inset*, 6 top*, 8*, 26*); Julien Hautcoeur/Shutterstock.com (4); Carol Highsmith/Library of Congress* (5, ); Edward Curtis/Library of Congress (6*, 7*); Frederic Remington (9*); C. Duhem & Bro./Library of Congress (10*); United States Congress (11*); Peter Newark's American Pictures (12); National Archives (13*, 25*); Carlisle Indian School Digital Resource Center (15); North Wind Picture Archives (16); U.S. Department of the Interior (17*); C.C. Pierce/USC (18*); Corbis (19 top, 20, 21, 25); Sotheby's (19 bottom); Poetry Foundation (22); U.S. Department of Energy (24); Paul Thompson/Photolibrary/Getty Images (28); Navajo Nation Council (29).

Cover images (clockwise from top: United States Congress*; Carol Highsmith/Library of Congress*; Corbis; C. Duhem & Bro./Library of Congress*; Library of Congress*; National Archives*.

*These images are in the public domain.

Cataloging-in-Publication Data
Names: Stewart, Mark, 1960 July 7-.
Title: Navajo history and culture / Mark Stewart.
Description: Buffalo, NY : Cavendish Square Publishing, 2026. | Series: In focus: Native Americans | Includes glossary and index.
Identifiers: ISBN 9781502675033 (pbk.) | ISBN 9781502675040 (library bound) | ISBN 9781502675057 (ebook)
Subjects: LCSH: Navajo Indians--Juvenile literature. | Indians of North America--Juvenile literature. | Indigenous peoples--Social life and customs--Juvenile literature.
Classification: LCC E99.N3 S94 2026 | DDC 979.10049726--dc23

CPSIA compliance information: Batch #CS26CSQ: For further information contact Cavendish Square Publishing LLC at 1-877-980-4450.
Printed in the United States of America

# CONTENTS



### ABOUT OUR GLOSSARY

In this book, there may be several words or terms you are reading for the first time, or words that are familiar but used in an unusual way. All of these words appear in **bold type** throughout the book and are defined on page 30.

# I AM THE LAND

The high desert of the American Southwest is a land of dramatic beauty, with soaring mesas and deep canyons carved by streams over millions of years. Every drop of water in this **arid** land is precious; the animals and humans who live there have learned how to make the most of what the environment has to

A Navajo girl poses for a photo in traditional clothing during the early 1900s.

Monument Valley provides a dramatic setting for three members of the Navajo tribe, who are also wearing traditional clothing.

offer. The Navajo people live on about 250,000 acres that stretch across New Mexico, Arizona, and southern Utah. However, they are not the first people to call this part of the world home.

The Pueblo people and their ancestors lived in this region for more than 1,000 years before the Navajo arrived. They built large settlements and learned how to farm the land, even in the most challenging of times. Based on the Navajo language, scholars believe that they

◀ The high desert home of the Navajo people includes Monument Valley, on the border of Arizona and Utah.

Navajo weavers are world famous for their work. They acquired this skill centuries ago.

came to New Mexico from the north, perhaps as far away as western Canada. They were a **semi-nomadic** people who had learned how to **adapt** to different environments and were not afraid to incorporate the skills of other tribes they encountered along the way.

From their new neighbors, the Pueblos, they added farming to their survival skills. In fact, the name "Navajo" comes from the Pueblo word *navahu'u*, which means "farm fields in the valleys." The Navajos were

also longtime neighbors of the Apaches, a tribe with whom they once shared many similarities. When Spanish explorers and settlers arrived in the region, they recognized these similarities and initially called the Navajo people *Apaches de Nabajó*. Members of the Navajo tribe called themselves *Diné*, or "the people."

The Spanish introduced the weaving of **textiles** to the Pueblos, which the Navajos quickly learned. The Navajos acquired sheep from Spanish settlers, which fit perfectly with their lifestyle and provided wool for their textile production.

With the arrival of Spanish settlers came horses, which made the Navajos more mobile.

In recent years, evidence has emerged of human presence in North America much earlier than previously thought—perhaps as long as 30,000 years ago. The northern ice sheet would have been impenetrable at that time, meaning that these people would have arrived by sea. Were the Navajos descendants of these early arrivals? Genetic research may one day provide an answer.

# FIRST CONTACT

Spanish explorers first arrived on the edge of Navajo territory in 1540, but it would be another 43 years before an expedition led by Antonio de Espejo reported meeting a tribe that lived in the mountains west of the Rio Grande River and who traded with the Pueblo townspeople. Spanish settlers arrived a generation later and attacked Navajo villages, killing the men and enslaving women and children. The Navajo retaliated by raiding Spanish ranches. During these raids, they took cattle and sheep, as well as horses. Soon the Navajos

This painting shows the arrival of Spanish forces in the 1540s. Decades of conflict followed.

became expert horsemen, which enabled them to resist Spanish attacks and avoid some of the diseases that **decimated** other tribes in the region.

Spain, and later Mexico, were unable to control the Navajos. In 1848, the United States defeated Mexico in a war and acquired over 500,000 square miles (1.3 million sq km) of territory, including Navajo lands. The U.S. Army built forts to protect American settlers and seized Navajo grazing land for their livestock. When the tribe fought back, the government launched a program to subdue them. During the 1860s, soldiers burned houses, destroyed crops, killed livestock, and chopped down fruit trees. Many Navajos fled west, while about 8,000 surrendered. They were forced to march 300 miles (483 km) across New Mexico to the Bosque Redondo prison camp. This became known as the "Navajo Long Walk."

This photo was taken during the "Long Walk," when thousands of Navajos were forced to march 300 miles by the U.S. Army.

# I AM A WARRIOR

Navajo warriors were taught from an early age how to ride, shoot, and engage in hand-to-hand combat. They knew every inch of their environment and specialized in setting traps and launching ambushes on their enemies. Their expertise in tracking animals meant they could observe the movements of their enemies without being seen. Navajo boys were trained to have great **stamina** and **endurance** and were able to cover long distances on foot or on horseback. Developing these skills was part of the "Navajo Way" and were highly prized whether attacking or defending their territory.

Although large battles sometimes occurred, most conflicts took the form of raids. Resources were scarce

This photo shows a Navajo warrior identified as "Jim" with a bow and arrows. He also has a horn to keep gunpowder dry.

Two Navajo warriors are shown in this illustration with long spears called lances.

in the desert Southwest and the Navajos targeted Spanish, Mexican, and American settlers, whom they felt were uninvited guests on their land. They also raided neighboring tribes, including the Apaches, Pueblos, and Hopis. Often these raids were part of years-long cycles of revenge and retaliation.

After Navajo lands came under control of the United States in the 1840s, many tribe members believed it was time to make peace with Americans. During a treaty meeting in 1849, an argument over a horse led to

the killing of Narbona, an influential Navajo chief. The incident convinced the Navajos to follow war leaders like Manuelito, Narbona's son-in-law, in opposing the U.S. military. They fought American settlers and soldiers for more than a decade.

During this period, several attempts were made to hammer out peace treaties, but none lasted long. The Navajos did not have a **central government**, so there were always groups that refused to accept terms. Also, years of mistrust between the Navajo people and Americans meant small disputes sometimes exploded into violence.

The skill and courage of Navajo soldiers would prove valuable to the United States during World War II, when they used a code based on their language to send radio messages to the front lines. Navajo grammar is complex and U.S. enemies were never able to crack the code. Other Native Americans—including Comanches and Hopis—also performed this vital and extremely dangerous duty. These soldiers were known as "code talkers."

◀ Manuelito led Navajo opposition to the U.S. government for many years before signing a peace treaty in 1868.

# A NEW REALITY

In 1868, the United States government released the prisoners from Bosque Redondo. They were allowed to return to land set aside for a Navajo reservation in New Mexico and supplied with sheep to rebuild their flocks. Beginning in the 1880s, hundreds of Navajo children were forced to attend boarding schools far from home. They were made to abandon their language and religion, and learn trades that were viewed as being suitable for fitting into the white world. This created massive disruption to Navajo culture.

Navajo reservation lands were increased several times in the 1800s and 1900s. Today the Navajo Nation covers 27,000 square miles (70,000 sq km), making it the largest reservation in the country. However, that is less than 15 percent of the tribe's original territory. The reservation is located in parts of New Mexico, Arizona, and Utah. It completely surrounds the reservation land of the Hopis, historic opponents of the Navajo people. This has led to decades of disputes.

A Navajo teenager named Tom Torling is shown in 1882, when he entered the government boarding school in Carlisle, Pennsylvania. The image on the right shows Tom three years later.

As a semi-nomadic people, the Navajos found the idea of a formal government **impractical**. The structure and rules of their **clans** had served them well for centuries, so they saw no need to change after their forced relocation. However, when oil was discovered on their land in 1921, the U.S. Department of the Interior insisted on a more organized form of government so that oil and gas **leases** could be signed.

# BEING NAVAJO

For humans to thrive in a challenging **ecosystem**, they must develop a deep understanding of—and connection to—the world around them. The Navajo succeeded for centuries as a semi-nomadic people. They followed the seasons to make the most of wild plants and animals, while farming the valleys and using pastureland to graze their livestock. Navajo farmers raised corn, beans, and squash—also commonly known as the "Three Sisters."

Their expertise in breeding sheep was central to tribal life. Sheep supplied wool, milk, and meat—all of which could be traded with neighboring tribes and settlers. Navajo-Churro sheep have two coats of long **fleece**, making it easy to work with. They also produce milk high in cream content. More than that, sheep came to symbolize harmony with nature.

The primary dwelling of the Navajos was the hogan. It was made of wood, stones, and packed earth, and usually eight-sided. Families typically built one in the

This photo shows two examples of hogans. In both cases, the entry faces toward the rising sun.

mountains, where they spent the summer months, and another in the valleys, where they spent their winters. In both cases, hogans performed brilliantly as energy-efficient structures—with ventilation in warm weather and thick walls to hold in the heat of a fire in cold weather. In both cases, the hogan's single door faced east toward the rising sun.

Traditional Navajo families are matrilineal, meaning that a woman is the head of the household and owner of the family's property. When a son married, he went to live with (or near) his wife's family. Navajo girls grew up with the understanding that they might one day be responsible for leading their family. That being said, neither gender was considered to be more important than the other.

Clans have served as the social and cultural structure of Navajo life for countless centuries. They provided members with rules of behavior called "walking in beauty." Even when separated by hundreds of miles, members of the same clan regarded one another as part of an extended family. Within a Navajo family, a mother's eldest brother was given great responsibility in raising her children. In tribal politics, men represented their mother's clan. From four ancient "original" clans, more than 100 clans now include Navajo members.

Navajo weavers tended to work outdoors, where it was cooler and brighter.

Navajo weavers have been part of the tribe's spiritual and economic life for hundreds of years. A weaver believes that her soul is part of every rug, blanket, and article of clothing she produces. Today, a Navajo weaver often will purposely include a small mistake in her design, as a reminder that it has been made by a human, not a machine.

This photo shows a Navajo man wearing a traditional warrior's headdress and a silver earring.

# SOMETHING SACRED

Throughout their history, the Navajo people have conducted many different religious and spiritual ceremonies. Most are associated with healing and often included a complex series of songs and rituals. Almost all had the goal of *hozho*—achieving or restoring a state of balance and harmony. According to Navajo tradition, being out of harmony causes illness. Many ceremonies involved Changing Woman, who is a **nurturing** figure in the tribe's creation myth. She represents **fertility**, rebirth, and the changing seasons. Changing Woman is still an important symbol for Navajo women.

A Navajo woman participates in the Spring Snow ceremony during the 1960s. It is one of many spiritual traditions that date back many centuries.

Ceremonies involving sand paintings are believed to connect the earthly and spirit worlds.

Identifying the correct healing ceremony to address an illness was the responsibility of the Hand Trembler. He would use hand **tremors** to diagnose the cause and then recommend a specific ceremony, which would usually be conducted by a medicine man or medicine woman, who combined spiritual and scientific beliefs. Some ceremonies involved sand paintings, which were believed to provide a path between the earthly and spirit worlds. The person being healed sat in the middle of the sand painting, and the illness was transferred to the painting, which was destroyed. Many Navajo healing ceremonies lasted a week or more and are still being performed.

The words associated with these ceremonies are astonishing works of poetry. The names of their original creators have been lost to time, but the tradition of Navajo literature is alive and well. Luci Tapahonso learned English as a second language growing up on a Navajo reservation. Because her work is a translation from Navajo to English, it retains the unusual **syntax** of Navajo grammar. In 2013, Tapahonso was the first person to be honored as **Poet Laureate** of the Navajo Nation.

The second, Laura Tohe, is the daughter of a Navajo code talker who was punished in school as a young girl for speaking Navajo. Her work has been translated into multiple languages. Vee F. Browne-Yellowhair is a writer and illustrator of children's books featuring traditional Navajo stories and characters. Her work also includes short stories. In 2025, she published her first young adult novel, entitled *The Ground Mist Girl.*

◀ Laura Tohe, an author and educator, was named Navajo Nation Poet Laureate in 2015. Her work includes a book about her experiences at a Native American boarding school.

# PAST, PRESENT, FUTURE

With more than 400,000 people enrolled, Navajo Nation now rivals the Cherokee Nation as the largest in the United States. Its capital is located in Window Rock, in northeastern Arizona, near the New Mexico state line. The Navajo Nation Council is the national **legislature** of the Navajo people. For many years, the council was controlled by a tribal chairman. Since 1990, they have elected a president to lead them.

Peterson Zah was an important Navajo leader in the 1990s.

The first was Peterson Zah, who some called the "Navajo Kennedy" (referring to U.S. president John F. Kennedy). Zah improved the tribe's economy and tackled complicated environmental issues, including

A Navajo girl takes part in a traditional ceremony. The Navajos place great importance on preserving their language and culture.

hundreds of abandoned **uranium** mines. He created the Permanent Fund, which set aside money from taxes on energy companies and other businesses operating on reservation lands. That money was used to build roads, create scholarships for students, and provide services to the elderly and disabled.

While many Native American tribes struggle to preserve their language and culture, the Navajo people have managed to protect theirs. More than 200,000 speak Navajo, both on and off reservation lands. Unfortunately, they share many of the problems that are part of reservation life across the United States. Rates

of poverty are high, and the Navajo people suffer from serious health issues at a much higher level than other American citizens.

For the better part of a century, the Navajo Nation economy depended on exploiting its natural resources, including oil, gas, coal, and uranium. They benefitted major cities such as Phoenix and Los Angeles, and created jobs for Navajo workers. However, extracting these resources from the earth generated air and water pollution, and left scars on Navajo land. For a culture that prizes balance and harmony, these decisions have come at a particularly high cost.

Preserving Navajo culture is done in many ways, including the preparation of traditional foods. This woman demonstrates how fry bread is made.

Other economic opportunities on the reservation include traditional work, such as ranching of sheep and cattle, weaving and other creative arts, and pockets of

A Navajo man makes a recording of his voice in 1914. Recordings like this are a valuable part of preserving the language.

agriculture. Tourism has become an important source of jobs since Navajo voters approved casinos on reservation land. The first opened in 2008 and several more are in operation. About $10 million from casino profits now goes directly to the reservation's 100-plus chapters.

When the Navajo Nation formed a formal government in the 1920s, a major challenge was its sheer size. With poor roads and communication infrastructure, it was impossible for every person to have a voice in matters of importance. The solution was to set up five agencies made up of dozens of chapters—each with its own house. There are now more than 100 Chapter Houses, where people can make decisions about local matters and also let their opinions be known through Navajo Nation delegates.

◀ Monument Valley Navajo Tribal Park features sandstone towers hundreds of feet high. More than 400,000 people visit every year, providing another important source of income.

# GLOSSARY AND FURTHER READING

## GLOSSARY

**Adapt**—Adjust in response to new opportunities or conditions.

**Arid**—Having almost no rain.

**Central Government**—A political system with a primary governing body.

**Clans**—Close-knit extended family related by kinship or common ancestors.

**Decimated**—Destroyed a large percentage.

**Ecosystem**—A group of living and non-living things that create nutrients and energy within an area.

**Endurance**—The ability to do something difficult for a long time.

**Fertility**—The natural ability for people, plants, and animals to reproduce.

**Fleece**—The woolly covering of a sheep.

**Impractical**—Not sensible or realistic.

**Leases**—Agreements that give certain rights to others in exchange for payment.

**Legislature**—A group of people who pass laws for a government.

**Nurturing**—Protecting and taking care of something that is growing.

**Poet Laureate**—A poet who is officially recognized by a government or organization, who often composes work for special occasions.

**Semi-Nomadic**—A lifestyle that includes settled communities in addition to seasonal migration.

**Stamina**—The ability to keep from tiring.

**Syntax**—The arrangement of words that create a sentence.

**Textiles**—Woven fabrics.

**Tremors**—Involuntary shaking of a hand or other body part.

**Uranium**—A radioactive metal that is found in small quantities in rocks.

## BOOKS


Krupat, Arnold. *Boarding School Voices: Carlisle Indian School Students Speak*. Lincoln, NE: University of Nebraska Press, 2021.

Rossiter, Brienna. *The Trail of Tears*. Mendota Heights, MN: North Star Editions, 2025.

Tyler, Ron. *Native Americans: The Complete Plates of McKenney, Catlin, and Bodmer*. Cologne, Germany: Taschen America, 2024.

Various Authors. *My Life: Growing Up Native in America*. New York, NY: MTV Books/Simon & Schuster Children's Publishing, 2024.


# ABOUT THE AUTHOR

**MARK STEWART** has written more than 150 non-fiction books for educational publishers, covering history, sports, and popular culture. His family tree tells a complex story common to many Americans. Mark's ancestors include some of the first European colonists, as well as the Indigenous people with whom early settlers interacted. Some faced off on the field of battle while others fought side-by-side. His 10th great-grandfather was **Myles Standish**, an officer on the *Mayflower*, while his ninth great-grandmother was **Singing Bird Corbison**, who was described as a "Shawnee woman" but who was probably from the **Wampanoag** tribe. The Wampanoag people saved Standish and his fellow **Pilgrims** from starvation during the winter of 1620–21, forming the basis for the story of Thanksgiving. The descendants of Corbison and Standish blended into a single family in 1789, and then headed west in search of opportunity. This brought Mark's ancestors into direct conflict with Native people along the frontier in the 1700s and 1800s. Mark's sixth great-grandmother recalled frantically casting bullets for her husband as they defended their small Kentucky fort from an attack. Another served under 23-year-old **Abraham Lincoln** in the Illinois Militia during the Black Hawk War of 1832. Mark's more recent ancestors chose to fight their battles with words—as writers and editors of books, newspapers, and magazines. In 2007, he authored a history of the **Indian Removal Act of 1830** and the infamous **Trail of Tears**.

# INDEX